Praise for
A Life Embraced

"Through the fifty-four years Bill and I served together in ministry, the support role I held was challenging and rewarding. Gayle's voice of experience reminds us that God values a wife's ministry of everyday responsibilities as much as he values a pastor's ministry. *A Life Embraced* reminds us that being a wife in ministry is a rewarding privilege."

> —VONETTE BRIGHT, cofounder, Campus Crusade for
> Christ, International

"I was thrilled to read this practical book that gives insight as it relates to accepting the call God predestined for us in the midst of the realities of life and ministry. For every pastor's wife and those aspiring to be, this is a must-read."

> —LOIS EVANS, DHL, senior vice president of The
> Urban Alternative and president of Global Pastors
> Wives Network

"*A Life Embraced* is a breath of hope to every woman who wonders if she has what she needs to make it! Gayle's transparent style is disarming as she shares the assurance that the Father not only sees you but desires to meet your deepest longings as you labor in his field."

> —LISA BEVERE, speaker and best-selling author of
> *Kissed the Girls and Made Them Cry*

"I would encourage any pastor's wife to read *A Life Embraced*. With sound advice regarding home, relationships, and family, it also touches a great deal on the partnership of marriage and how important that is for a healthy, successful ministry."

—ANNA M. HAYFORD, wife of pastor Jack W. Hayford

"I have seen that the demands of a pastor's wife can be overwhelming *unless* she has been given solid biblical ways to deal with the challenges. Gayle Haggard has recognized this tremendous need and is meeting it. This book will be a blessing to pastors' wives and the wives of evangelists, youth pastors, and so on. At our husband's side, we have a tremendous opportunity to change the world for God's glory."

—EVELYN ROBERTS, wife of evangelist Oral Roberts

"During an age in which pastors' wives feel overworked, misunderstood, and alone, Gayle Haggard lovingly embraces and encourages each one. With warmth and wisdom, Gayle shares honestly from her own life and from God's Word."

—LORRAINE PINTUS, conference speaker and coauthor
of *Intimate Issues*

"In *A Life Embraced*, Gayle Haggard marries grace and truth, giving deep wisdom concerning every area of a wife's life. I highly recommend this book to every leader's wife."

—LINDA DILLOW, mission leader's wife and coauthor
of *Intimate Issues*

A *Life* EMBRACED

A Hopeful Guide for the Pastor's Wife

GAYLE HAGGARD
Foreword by DENALYN LUCADO

WATERBROOK
PRESS

To Ted—

You are the reason I love being a pastor's wife!

A LIFE EMBRACED
PUBLISHED BY WATERBROOK PRESS
2375 Telstar Drive, Suite 160
Colorado Springs, Colorado 80920
A division of Random House, Inc.

All Scripture quotations, unless otherwise indicated, are taken from the *Holy Bible, New International Version®*. NIV®. Copyright © 1973, 1978, 1984 by International Bible Society. Used by permission of Zondervan Publishing House. All rights reserved. Scripture quotations marked (NASB) are taken from the *New American Standard Bible* ® (NASB). © Copyright The Lockman Foundation 1960, 1962, 1963, 1968, 1971, 1972, 1973, 1975, 1977, 1995. Used by permission. (www.Lockman.org).

ISBN 1-4000-7062-7

Copyright © 2004 by Gayle Haggard

Library of Congress Cataloging-in-Publication Data
Haggard, Gayle.
A life embraced : a hopeful guide for the pastor's wife / Gayle Haggard.—1st ed.
    p. cm.
  ISBN 1-4000-7062-7
  1. Spouses of clergy—Religious life. 2. Haggard, Gayle. I. Title.
BV4395.H3 2004
253'.22—dc22   2004019709

Printed in the United States of America
2004—First Edition

10 9 8 7 6 5 4 3 2 1

Contents

a LifeGiving book

from TED HAGGARD & FRIENDS

Jesus said that He came to give His followers life—abundant life.

What an incredible promise—that any of us, regardless of the experiences of the past or the circumstances of the present, can tap into a rich, deep, never-ending supply of Jesus's *life!*

At New Life Church, we encourage the flow of this Christ-energized life into every individual and endeavor. We challenge our staff to produce life-giving ideas, life-changing messages, and life-saving advice that will equip our people to embrace the fullness of God's promises in relationships, family, small groups, church, community, and even the world.

This desire to seize all the life Jesus promised is why we joined in partnership with WaterBrook Press to produce LifeGiving Books—high-quality publications that deliver a refreshing and empowering sip of the abundant living water Christ gives to those who earnestly seek and follow Him.

Welcome to another LifeGiving Book! God bless you as you read.

Here's to *Life!*

—Pastor Ted Haggard
New Life Church, Colorado Springs

Acknowledgments

To Liz Heaney, my editor: You are a godsend! This couldn't have happened without you. Thank you for teaching me and pushing me to tell my stories.

To Don Pape at WaterBrook: You heard me and gave me a great title. Thanks for all your encouragement!

To my friends Aileen, Julie, and Julia: "A cord of three strands is not quickly broken." You were a steady source of strength and joy to me every week.

To my niece Carolyn: Thank you for coming alongside to help and for all your thoughtful encouragement!

To Lance and Rachel, who created a beautiful place for me to write and encouraged me from the start: Thank you!

To the receptionists and hospitality staff at the World Prayer Center: Thank you for your prayers and for cheerfully caring for me.

To all my friends who prayed for me and encouraged me along the way—Marky Gilbert, Doris West, Sherron

Hudson, Elizabeth Miller, Karen Duncan-Flanagan, Joanne Thompson, and Gloria Gildea, to mention a few: Thank you!

To Linda Dillow and Lorraine Pintus: Thank you for your wise insights and prayers and for cheering me on!

To Lisa Bevere: What a welcome surprise your encouraging phone calls were!

To Lori Vafiades: Thank you for inspiring me with your lovely painting, *The Harvesters,* which appears on the cover of this book.

To my children, Christy, Marcus, Jonathan, Alex, and Elliott: You were my joy at the end of the day. Thank you for sacrificing and supporting me. Mom's home now!

To New Life Church: You make being a pastor's wife easy. Oh, that every church could be like you. You make Ted and me love what we do!

To Ted: You are the reward! I love being your wife and embracing the life God has given us together.

Foreword

Those who read *A Life Embraced* will find a new friend in Gayle Haggard. She writes honestly and transparently, painting a very real picture of life, not a rose-tinted one. Her wise words will bless any woman, whether she is married to a pastor, a plumber, or a psychologist. For, as Gayle points out, "all God requires of any of us is a sincere heart, a teachable spirit, and, of course, obedience." I love that!

As Gayle shares the many lessons God has taught her about how to experience true freedom and joy, you will see evidence of God's faithfulness. When she felt disappointed that her husband wasn't giving her enough attention because of his responsibilities as a pastor, God gently showed her the depth of His love for her. When she struggled with wanting to be alongside her husband on the "front lines" of ministry, God whispered to her, "I see you," and assured her that her work at home was just as important to Him as was her husband's work with their congregation. This book contains story after story about how God has guided Gayle as she has learned to depend on Him more and more for direction and insight.

Along with Gayle, I can say that dependence on the Lord has freed me as a person, a wife, and a mom. I have always naturally wanted to please people, and as the wife of a very visible person, I have many people in my life whom I could try to please. This continues to be a challenge for me, but I find myself praying more and more, *Let me be a God-pleaser, not a people-pleaser.* That's why I so appreciated Gayle's instruction to keep a strong relationship with God. When we seek to please Him first, other priorities will fall in line. If you are married to a leader, you are always being watched. Use that reality as a chance to pray more and be in God's Word. Press into Him, and He will be glorified in your life.

My heart resonates with Gayle's as she talks about how much she loves being a mom. God has given my husband, Max, and me three precious gifts: Jenna, Andrea, and Sara. Our daughters were young when we took the pastorate at

Oak Hills. I, like Gayle, felt a huge desire to protect them from the stares and glares and expectations of the church. This has been an important commitment for Max and me. We have done our best to help each other in this, and the Lord has been faithful. Through the ups and downs of life, He has kept His hand on our family. He goes before us, comes up behind us, and walks beside us.

More than anything, God wants us to know Him and who we are in Christ. When our sufficiency is found in Jesus Christ, then we are freed up to be who God wants us to be. This is a common theme in *A Life Embraced.* It's evident that Gayle has learned, step by step, to depend completely on the Lord. She, like the rest of us, has experienced God's mercy as He has patiently called her to Himself.

Years ago I went through a season when I battled depression. Those dark days were difficult at best and challenging at least. Yet through them I experienced the truth of Jesus's words when He promised, "My grace is sufficient for you, for my power is made perfect in weakness" (2 Corinthians 12:9). In that darkness God was calling my name, asking me to lean on Him. I look back on that time in my life and see it now as God's severe mercy. The depression was harsh, but God used it to mercifully reveal to me His power and beauty. I now know and believe with all my heart that I cannot take one step or one breath without Jesus—nor do I want to. Only He can satisfy my soul.

The Lord has a life for you and me to embrace. With Jesus, that life is abundant, regardless of our circumstances. I pray that God will use the words of Gayle Haggard to give you a portion of what you need. As you read, don't hesitate to pause and remember your own stories and God's mighty work in your life. You may even want to stop and pray or worship. If life is tough, hold on. If life is great, be thankful.

—DENALYN LUCADO

Finding Happiness

I love being a pastor's wife. Over the last twenty-five years, my husband has been a youth pastor and a pastor with a congregation of thirty-five, one hundred, one thousand, and now, more than eleven thousand people. As the church has grown, I have grown, and somewhere along the way, I learned to embrace with joy this life God has given me.

This hasn't always been true. I can't say I loved being a pastor's wife when Ted and I were first married. Even though I said I loved my role, I was filled with fear. I wasn't sure I could live up to all the expectations our congregation might have of me. I feared I wouldn't have the right answers, that I didn't know enough Scripture, and I was terrified that I might have to speak publicly.

But I've learned a few things since those early days. I am no longer afraid of my role or of whether I can do it. Instead, I have learned that being a pastor's wife boils down to these two things: growing up in God and helping others do the same. As I've learned to lean heavily on the Word of God and the counsel of the Holy Spirit, I have gained confidence and freedom because I know that all God requires of any of us is a sincere heart, a teachable spirit, and, of course, obedience.

Life as a pastor's wife can be as hard or as easy as we make it, depending on how quickly we respond to the voice of the Holy Spirit, our Teacher and Counselor. Being a pastor's wife is all about simply being a Christian. After all, that is what got us into this position in the first place. We were believers of God, and we fell in love with and married men who were also believers. Somewhere along the way, God called our husbands to be pastors, and so we became pastors' wives.

In this book I hope to encourage you on this journey. I want you to know that you can have a bright future as a pastor's wife.

On a wall of the room where I wrote this book hangs a painting that captures the vision I have for pastors' wives and for Christian women everywhere. It colorfully depicts a group of women joyously bringing in the harvest, their arms and faces uplifted. Even though the artist didn't paint their faces, I can tell these women are smiling. They exude joy and celebration. They are happy. Free. Fulfilled. This is my vision for all of us.

Perhaps you are young and full of hope but also a little afraid as I was, wondering if you are up to the task of being a pastor's wife. Or maybe you've been married to a pastor for a while, yet you're still fearful or even discouraged. Or perhaps you are one of the many pastors' wives who are burned out—your hopes are already shattered, and your future looks bleak. Or maybe you are among those who have figured out how to embrace your role. Regardless of where you are today, you need to know that God has a good plan for you and wants you to be happy, yes, *happy,* as a pastor's wife.

Some of us are suspicious of the word *happy* because we think pursuing happiness means being frivolous and lacking maturity and spiritual depth. But the kind of happiness I am talking about goes far deeper than a surface type of giggly exuberance or even a sense of well-being based on positive circumstances. It goes beyond momentary laughter—although laughter is good—and is more real than a superficial appearance of peace and contentment. When I think of being happy, I imagine the Proverbs 31 woman who "smiles at the future" (verse 25, NASB). This woman has something substantive hidden within her heart that causes her to smile and gives her strength. She faces life with joy and looks forward, happily and without fear, to her future.

I feel this about my life now because I have learned a few truths about life and walking with God that have brought me through the many circumstances and challenges that life and ministry have presented. In this book I will share them with you. Whether you are suffering under heavy burdens associated with your role or just want to know how to be a great pastor's wife, I think these truths can help you.

For too long pastors' wives have borne the image of women overburdened with expectations and limitations, and living under a microscope. Many see us as being set apart and lonely, and they feel pity toward us even while trying to show appreciation for our roles. There is something terribly wrong with this picture. This isn't how it should be, nor is it what God intends for us. He wants us to be happy. I am not talking about pursuing happiness; I am talking about *receiving* it. Did you know the word *bless* means to make happy? We all know that God desires to bless us, so this means He wants to make us happy—fulfilled, satisfied at our core, women who are able to smile at the future.

This doesn't mean we won't have hardship and difficulties in our lives. The Scriptures teach us that we will. I certainly do. One of my greatest challenges is having a disabled son with whom I've shared much struggle and heartache. We will all experience pain and sadness to some degree; suffering will surround us. It is inescapable if we live on the earth very long. We may also experience discipline from our Father who loves us. Such challenges can contribute to our maturity.

The happiness I'm referring to isn't pain-free bliss. I am talking about a substantive happiness at our core that can't be shaken, no matter what our circumstances. This is what God intends for us. As pastors' wives, we need this. Every Christian does.

When you think about happiness, think about the

delight happy children bring to their parents. Would you feel any pleasure if your children went around with sad faces, thinking life was all about duty, that it was just hard and monotonous? I don't think so. As parents we feel deep satisfaction when our children are happy. It announces to the world that we are good parents. The same is true of our heavenly Father. He delights in the happy contentment of His children, and our happiness announces to the world that He is a good Father. He takes no pleasure in our carrying unnecessary burdens. Remember, His yoke is easy and His burden is light (Matthew 11:30). He came to set us free (John 8:36 and Galatians 5:1) and to give us hope (Ephesians 1:18-19).

Our happiness as pastors' wives includes experiencing the freedom Jesus has provided for us. We can experience freedom from the day-to-day heaviness that sin and demonic schemes create. We can also walk free of unbiblical expectations, trying to please everyone, because we know it is God we should be seeking to please, which will ultimately enable us to serve others better.

When I think of being free, I imagine my favorite

vacation scenario. I see myself floating on gently rolling ocean waves, my hair swirling slowly around my head, the sun shining down on my face—and I can't help but smile. Freedom for me is a return to innocence, childlikeness, and unencumbered delight. That's freedom. People who are truly free have a purity about them. They encourage your heart. They lift you up. They make you smile. You want to be with them and look at them. Why? Because the burdens they carry don't weigh them down, and, consequently, they don't weigh you down either.

How can we possibly achieve this kind of freedom as pastors' wives?

I think I've found a way.

I start by remembering that God sent Jesus to set me free and that He is delighted when I receive His gifts. Sure, I don't spend my days floating on the ocean. I don't even live near an ocean. I have plenty to do every day. I am a wife and a mom of five children, one of whom, as I mentioned, is disabled. Our church has eleven thousand members, and I oversee our women's ministry. But I carry this freedom with me, and it makes me smile.

Every morning when I read God's Word and pray, the Holy Spirit counsels me and shows me the things I must deal with in my heart so that I can continue to float, not sink, in my ocean of freedom in Him. During this time He gives me the ideas I need so that I can do what He's given me to do without feeling overwhelmed. My time with Him, hearing His voice and receiving His counsel, is my source of strength, and it can be yours as well. I am confident this source of strength is available to all of us who believe.

Spending time with God did not come easily to me, however. I spent years trying to discipline myself into daily Bible reading and prayer. For many years, particularly when our children were small, most of my attempts ended in failure. I would start a new plan to read through the Bible in a year, and three weeks later I would already be behind several chapters. I've read Genesis more than any book in the Bible, and I know I am not alone in this.

Prayer was even harder. I tried to set aside an hour to pray every day, but my prayer time would be constantly interrupted. I struggled to focus and often ended up writing grocery lists and to-do lists for the day instead of praying.

I remember one such morning when I was trying to steal away for a few minutes of quiet. I had settled on the sofa with my Bible open, when my then three-year-old son Marcus marched in, asking me to help him find his treasured cowboy hat. I knew this was a matter of urgent importance to him and that a simple "Honey, run along, and I will help you later" wouldn't do. But I didn't want to give up yet on my quiet time, so I suggested that he pray about it and ask God to help him find his cowboy hat.

The next time I looked up, I noticed Marcus standing in the middle of the living room, staring straight up at the ceiling. I asked him what he was doing, and he said he was asking God where his cowboy hat was. After a moment he looked back at me, and I asked him if God had answered. He said, "Yes, but He says He doesn't know where it is either." Okay, so that was pretty precious. None of us wants to lose such moments with our children. Yet each of us desperately needs time alone with God, even if we have to learn how to do this in the presence of our loved ones.

So because I believed that prayer and Bible study are necessary for a strong Christian life, I kept on trying. Then one day I broke through. Somehow in the midst of all my defeated attempts, it occurred to me that God had sent His Holy Spirit to teach me, counsel me, and guide me. So I started to talk to Him about my desire to walk with Him and know Him more, and before long, not only was I able to fill an hour with prayer, but my days were filled with prayer. I would think about God as I went about my tasks. Throughout the day I talked to Him about many things. Sometimes I would sense His gentle nudging and quiet voice in my spirit, responding to me and instructing me.

I then began to recognize in me this thirst for His Word. I couldn't wait to get up in the morning to read it, whether it was just a few verses or several chapters, and the more I read, the more I reflected on what I was reading, and the more the Holy Spirit spoke to me and counseled me. If you have not yet entered into this type of relationship with the Holy Spirit, make it your goal and don't give up, even if you meet with failure time and again. God comes near to those who come near to Him (James 4:8) and those who seek Him will find Him (Proverbs 8:17). You will eventually break through.

As pastors' wives, we need this private time with God. It refreshes us, leads to freedom in our hearts, and is the key to happiness in life and ministry.

For those of you who think I am being a little simplistic, I admit I am. But I have discovered that the richest, most rewarding wisdom is simple. We just have to do it. And that is where the problem lies. Many times we know what to do; we just don't do it. We embark on sophisticated detours that take us way off track. After twenty-five years of being a pastor's wife, I have learned that happiness comes from hearing the voice of the Holy Spirit and receiving His counsel—and then doing what He tells me to do.

If His voice is unfamiliar to you, you can best learn to hear it by reading the Bible as often and as much as you can. If you do, you will become familiar with the kinds of things God says and will be able to recognize His voice when He is speaking to you. As you read the Word, ponder it, pray about it, and let the Holy Spirit teach you. Sometimes when I am reading the Word, He says things to me that have nothing to do with what I am reading. I believe this happens because during my time with Him, I'm intentionally listening for His voice. He sometimes shows me things in my heart that He wants to clean up, things I may not even have been aware of. Occasionally He surprises me with a totally new idea or task He wants me to do, which is how I got involved in women's ministry. Most of the time He encourages and comforts me.

If you learn to hear the voice of the Holy Spirit, you will be able to carry a sense of God's presence with you throughout the day. As He becomes your guide and comforts you, any anxiety you may feel about your role as a pastor's wife will slowly dissipate, and you will find freedom and happiness. Learn to walk with Him, and you will smile at your future.

---

*But the Counselor, the Holy Spirit, whom the Father will
send in my name, will teach you all things
and will remind you of everything I have said to you.*

—John 14:26

---

*But when he, the Spirit of truth, comes,
he will guide you into all truth.*

—John 16:13

The truth will set you free.

—John 8:32

2

Discovering True Intimacy

I f you are like me, when your husband asked you to marry him, you began dreaming that your married life and ministry would include lots of time devoted to studying the Scriptures and praying together and helping other people. You couldn't wait to develop that body-and-soul oneness with your husband that the Bible talks about. You looked forward to becoming a parent and raising your children in a peaceful, godly home. In other words, you dreamed of a romantic life, overflowing with shared intimacy as you served God together.

You probably heard stories of neglected pastors' families and life in a fishbowl, but somehow you imagined that your life would be different. I know I did. It didn't take long, however, for me to discover that being married to a pastor wasn't going to go quite the way I had planned.

When Ted and I first married, we worked in a mission organization and for a church. We worked primarily with the youth, but we were also involved at some level with everything the church was doing. I remember feeling that Ted's entire focus was on his work. It seemed as if he was going, going, gone all the time.

He, of course, had honorable intentions of establishing himself in ministry and doing an effective work. His focus was on serving God and the church well. My focus, on the other hand, was on establishing our relationship. Even though I loved our call into ministry and wanted to be involved in helping my husband, I could not let go of my desire for more time alone with him. I wanted my husband to spend more of his time sitting across the table looking deeply into my eyes and telling me how much he loved me and how wonderful he thought I was. And I wanted do the same for him—evening after evening after evening.

But we had very few of these evenings. And when they did happen, I was so love-starved (at least by my definition) that my crying and complaining about our never having enough time together would make a mess of things.

I have this lovely memory of myself standing at the door with a tear-streaked face and a red nose as I watched

Ted drive off. Our parting comments had gone something like this:

"Do you have to go again tonight? Can't you just stay home with me?"

"Honey, I have to go. John just found out his mother has a brain tumor, and she only has a month to live."

So as Ted raced off to help people and do great things for God, I stood at the door, waving good-bye and feeling ashamed of my selfishness.

I felt guilty, confused, and hurt. Within a few months of getting married, I began to believe that Ted and I were never going to have any intimacy or romance in our marriage. Heartbroken, I began to pray about my disappointment.

Understand, I loved what Ted was doing. I loved that he was so committed to God, and I respected his selflessness. I loved God, too. Nonetheless, I felt this huge need to be with my husband. I wanted us to spend as many intimate moments together as we could. In the midst of my desperation, the Lord started to speak to me during prayer. He told me that before I had married Ted, my heart and life were given to Him. But after our marriage, I had taken all of the devotion I had invested in my relationship with God and redirected it toward Ted. I longed for my husband to meet me at that same deeply intimate level and to fulfill all of my emotional needs, to be my constant companion to talk to and process life with. I just took that place in my heart that only the Lord had filled and gave it to Ted (what a present!), and I thought I was doing the right thing. I thought this was what a wife was supposed to do—that God, who had walked me through all my stages of life and spiritual growth up until that time, somehow intended for me to do this. But what He told me was that until I returned that most intimate place in my heart to Him, He was not going to give me the kind of intimacy in my marriage I longed for.

This came as a total shock. God wanted to change *me,* not Ted. I was the one who was off course. So I began a journey to become more intimate with my heavenly Father, and when I felt that longing for deep connection in my heart, I began to go to Him first rather than to Ted. When I felt hurt or neglected or selfish, I tried to immediately turn my attention to God and ask Him to help me. I would talk to Him about it and look into His Word, and He would counsel me.

As my intimacy with God deepened, I started thinking of Him as the Lover of my soul. Often I would wake up and say, "Good morning, Holy Spirit. You are the Lover of my soul. You are my dearest Friend. I thank You that I can talk to You about the deepest needs of my heart. You are my Teacher and Counselor." As I became more secure in my intimacy with Him, I became less clingy with Ted. I wasn't looking to him to fill all of my emotional and spiritual needs, something God never intended for him to do anyway.

I began to understand what the psalmist David was talking about when he said,

Because your love is better than life,
    my lips will glorify you....
On my bed I remember you;
    I think of you through the watches of the night.
Because you are my help,
    I sing in the shadow of your wings.

My soul clings to you;

    your right hand upholds me. (Psalm 63:3,6-8)

Of course, this change in me and in our marriage didn't happen overnight. It actually took place over a period of several years. I continued to try to grow in my relationship with Ted and to be a support to him, but I didn't look to him to fulfill the deepest needs of my heart. Even though he was my husband and a great friend and encourager, Ted could not see into my heart the way the Holy Spirit could. I couldn't see into Ted's heart either, as much as I wanted to. Neither of us could take the place of the Holy Spirit in each other's lives.

But as I learned to look to the Lord to meet my needs, I became much more pleasant to live with. God so satisfied me that I was able to turn my focus from my inward neediness to an outward participation in life and service with Ted. This was nothing short of a divine transformation of my person, and it led to greater intimacy in our marriage, which was what I had hoped for early on.

As I was growing more fulfilled and satisfied in God,

I was becoming increasingly attractive to my husband. Instead of seeing me as trying to hold him back with a sad face, tears, and a shaky voice every time he went out the door, he started seeing me as having it together and being supportive of him.

When we hit our thirties, "Hello romance!" and our intimacy started to blossom. Since that time we have connected on a much deeper level and have grown to love and understand each other better. But I have never forgotten the lesson the Lord taught me: *The love of a husband is icing on the cake, but it is not the cake. The cake is intimacy with God.*

When I stopped demanding intimacy from Ted and discovered intimacy with God, I became whole, which in turn made me more attractive to my husband, which led to greater intimacy with him. God delights in this type of relationship. It's His desire to make each of us whole, and only He can do this.

In the years since, I have discovered a few things about men and women that, had I known about them earlier, may have alleviated some of the heartache I felt early in our marriage. I have learned that most men in their twenties are focused on establishing themselves in their work. It is a driving force for them. They need to know they can be successful. This is especially true for pastors who are seeking God's affirmation as well as the affirmation of church leaders and those in their congregations. I have also learned that most women in their twenties, including pastors' wives, are more focused on establishing relationships and family. We want to know that our relationships are secure. Once men establish themselves in their work, they are more confident to focus on their relationships. Once women feel secure in their relationships, they are more confident to focus on their work.

Because I didn't understand this in the early years of my marriage, I suffered some unnecessary disappointment. Even so, I do not regret those years. They are what forced me into a more intimate relationship with the Holy Spirit, who guided me through them and through all these many years of being a pastor's wife since.

As I drew closer to God, my intimacy with Him became the foundation on which everything else He had to teach me would be built. It is what led to another transforming lesson that had a powerful impact on me in my early years as a pastor's wife. It gave me the confidence that God values my life, that I count to Him. Perhaps you are in need of this revelation...

Your love is better than life…. My soul clings to you;
your right hand upholds me.

—Psalm 63:3,8

3

Realizing There Is
One Who Sees You

When our children were young and Ted was busy with ministry, my life seemed filled with the mundane: day after day, doing the same laundry, washing the same dishes, cleaning up the same messes, and exhausting myself in trying to nurture and discipline our children. While I spent my days at home, caring for our children and managing our household, Ted spent his doing significant things for the kingdom.

One day I cried out to the Lord because I felt so left out of what Ted was doing. I felt called to help him in ministry as well as at home, and I wanted to share in his experiences. I wanted to travel with him, to meet the people he was meeting. I wanted my life to count. I wanted to make a difference in the world.

I loved my children and wanted to be with them, but I wanted to be with my husband, too, to grow with him and be involved in all God had called him to do. In that moment when I was crying out to God, the Holy Spirit surprised me and spoke something deep into my spirit. He told me, "I see you."

I see you.

These three simple words, which settled over me like a warm blanket, had a profound impact on me. They changed the way I saw my life. I wasn't as hidden away and left out of the picture as I had thought. God saw me. He saw me cleaning our house to make it a pleasant place for my husband and children to live; He saw me washing and folding clothes so my husband and children would have something to wear. At night when I was so tired I could hardly see, He saw me trying to read or tell stories to my children so they would feel secure and loved and have happy memories. He saw me carefully packing Ted's suitcase, making sure he would have everything he needed when he was traveling. God saw me loving and caring for my family.

When God told me, "I see you," He helped me begin to realize how big my life actually was and how important my contribution was to Ted's life. I started to see that everything I did, I could do "as for the Lord" (Colossians

3:23, NASB), and that it counted in God's eyes. Taking care of our children and creating a home for our family were important responsibilities, and my doing them well made it possible for Ted to do the things God had given him to do. In caring for our family and home, I was part of God's plan. This created a foundation of strength for my husband and was my God-given part of our ministry; I actually helped Ted's ability to lead and pastor the church and do everything else God was giving him to do.

Colossians 3:23-24 says, "Whatever you do, work at it with all your heart, as working for the Lord, not for men, since you know that you will receive an inheritance from the Lord as a reward. It is the Lord Christ you are serving." Understanding that God *sees* me, that He knows I am taking care of my family and home as for Him, and that He values this as important to helping my husband serve Him has made all the difference. I no longer dread the seemingly ordinary tasks I have to do, because my perspective has changed. What I do counts for eternity.

I am not the only one who needs to be seen. Everyone has this need. I believe God has given us this desire because He longs to be seen as well. He tells us repeatedly throughout the Bible to look for Him, to seek Him, and to find Him. Jeremiah 29:13 says this: "You will seek me and find me when you seek me with all your heart." Psalm 14:2 tells us, "The LORD looks down from heaven on the sons of men to see if there are any who understand, any who seek God." God longs for us to see Him and to know Him as He is. I believe this is one of the reasons He created us—and made us like Him.

We share with God this need to be known. Each of us longs for someone to see into our heart and really know us as we are, to see the good along with the bad, to see the best of our intentions, and to affirm that we have value. We want someone to see past our failures and recognize the desires of our heart.

Have you ever wished that someone could see the real you, the best you? That someone could see what was really in your heart, that someone would believe in the better part about you?

There is One who sees you, just as He saw Hagar.

In Genesis 16 we see her story unfold. She was Sarai's

maidservant. Years had passed since God had promised Abram he would have a son, yet Sarai had borne him no children. So, Sarai gave her servant, Hagar, to Abram to see if he could have a child through her. When Hagar knew that she was pregnant, she began to despise Sarai. This, of course, upset Sarai, so Abram gave her permission to do to Hagar whatever she thought best. Sarai began to mistreat Hagar, so Hagar fled into the desert.

The angel of the Lord found her there and told her to go back to her mistress and submit to her. He said that he would give her so many descendants that no one would be able to count them. Hagar must have been grateful for this affirmation that her life counted and awed that God had met with her. In response, she gave this name to the Lord: "You are the God who sees me" (verse 13). Keep in mind that Hagar was an Egyptian maidservant. In the eyes of others, she was not important. She was alone, husbandless, and was despised by her mistress. Yet God met her in the desert and revealed to her the significance of her life and His plan for her son and his descendants. God saw her.

God also saw Sarai. In Genesis 17 God confirmed His

covenant with Abram and changed Abram's name to Abraham. He also changed Sarai's name to Sarah. God was not just concerned with Abraham; His eyes were on Sarah as well. The name He gave her meant "princess," and this was how He saw her. Sometimes, when speaking to Abraham, God would tell him that Sarah had a part in all that He was sharing with him. When He changed Sarah's name, God told Abraham, "I will bless her and will surely give you a son by her. I will bless her so that she will be the mother of nations; kings of peoples will come from her" (verse 16). She had a part in Abraham's calling.

When the three visitors met with Abraham, they asked him, "Where is your wife Sarah?" (Genesis 18:9). Then, when the Lord told Abraham that his wife would have a son the next year, Sarah, who was listening from the tent, laughed. When the Lord asked why she had laughed, Sarah denied it because she was afraid. God had been watching her. She mattered to Him. In Genesis 21 we read that God did for Sarah what He had promised.

When God looked at Hagar, He saw a woman who needed help and encouragement. He gave her what she needed to care for her son, and He showed her that she and her son counted, that He had a plan for them.

When God looked at Sarah, He saw a princess. He even presented her as an example for women:

> For this is the way the holy women of the past
> who put their hope in God used to make them-
> selves beautiful. They were submissive to their
> own husbands, like Sarah, who obeyed Abraham
> and called him her master. You are her daughters
> if you do what is right and do not give way to fear.
> (1 Peter 3:5-6)

Despite her mistreatment of Hagar and her lies to God about laughing, God saw something beautiful in Sarah's heart, something that was precious to Him.

How does God see you? We all have a need to be seen, and it takes just one to see us to satisfy our hearts. There is a God in heaven who does. Psalm 139:1-3 says, "O LORD, you have searched me and you know me. You know when I sit and when I rise; you perceive my thoughts from afar. You discern my going out and my lying down; you are familiar with all my ways." If this isn't enough to convince you how well God knows you, just read the rest of this psalm. He doesn't miss a thing. When we really "get" this truth, it satisfies something deep within us and makes us feel valued to Him.

When things get tough and I am working through something I find difficult, I still find comfort in knowing God sees me. Even if no one else knows what I am going through, He does.

I've come to depend on this, particularly when it comes to relationships. One of the lessons I learned early on was how to receive the Holy Spirit's counsel in dealing with my own heart so that I could take the "plank" out of my own eye in order to see to "remove the speck" from someone else's (Matthew 7:3-5). In my experience, once I get the plank out of my own eye, I can't seem to find the speck in the other person's. But sometimes it takes real work to get the plank out of my own eye. The Holy Spirit is the only One who knows how hard it is for me, because this goes on privately where only He can see. He knows the strength of the judgments in my heart, and when I submit to Him and work with Him to clean up my heart and restore purity and innocence to it, He knows it. He knows because He sees me.

I have gone through this process so many times I've lost count. Judging other people just seems to come so easily to me. I used to think it was my ministry gift, but I've since learned how displeasing it is to our heavenly Father. So I go through the process time and again, and on the other side is a clean heart and innocence and freedom to love the people I once judged. God knows this about me. He sees me work these things out because of my desire to please Him.

So be encouraged, dear pastor's wife. Your life is of great value to God, and He sees every sacrifice and every endeavor to please Him and to be obedient to Him. Embrace whatever season of life you are in, knowing that each season matures you a little more and prepares you for the next. This is the path to wisdom if you submit to the God who sees you and are willing to learn the lessons He has for you along the way. It is how you can become like the excellent woman in Proverbs 31 who has faithful instruction on her tongue and laughs at the days to come.

You are the God who sees me.

—Genesis 16:13

O LORD, you have searched me and you know me. You know when I sit and when I rise; you perceive my thoughts from afar. You discern my going out and my lying down; you are familiar with all my ways.

—Psalm 139:1-3

4

Unveiling the Treasure
of Our Femininity

E very year I teach a class for the women of our church to help them understand what Scripture has to say about their unique value as women.* Over the years I've watched marriage relationships and relationships with children and parents be healed and friendships be restored, all because women begin to understand their God-given value and learn to appreciate their own femininity and value it in other women. Knowing we have inherent value satisfies something deep within us that sets us free from too much self-focus so we can focus on others and love them—and in doing so, become beautiful as women.

I want to share with you what I've discovered God says about our femininity that has brought priceless value to my life as a woman and has enhanced the way I see my role as a pastor's wife. Let's begin at the beginning and

---

* The study I use for this class is from Barbara Mouser, *Five Aspects of Woman: A Biblical Theology of Femininity* (Waxahachie, TX: International Council for Gender Studies, 1997).

return to the garden where the first revelation of woman unfolds:

> So God created man in his own image,
>> in the image of God he created him;
>> *male* and *female* he created *them*.
>
> God blessed *them* and said to *them,* "Be fruitful and increase in number; fill the earth and subdue it. Rule over the fish of the sea and the birds of the air and over every living creature that moves on the ground." (Genesis 1:27-28, emphasis added)

In this passage we learn that men and women are created equal in that we are both made in God's image and share God's command to rule over the earth. We have similar bodies and minds and abilities, and each of us is capable of ruling our worlds.

We find this equality supported again in Galatians 3:28-29, which says, "There is neither Jew nor Greek, slave nor free, *male nor female,* for you are all one in Christ Jesus. If you belong to Christ, then you are Abraham's seed, and heirs according to the promise" (emphasis added). In this verse we find that men and women are also equal in our ability to have relationships with God. We have equal access to Him and His promises. We are equally heirs.

This knowledge forms the foundation of our relationship as husband and wife. It should lead us to respect each other, appreciate each other's value, and recognize how very much we share in common. I reject the notion that men and women are so different that we can never understand each other. God made us to understand and know each other! When we acknowledge that we are more alike than we are different, it goes a long way toward improving our communication.

The problem is, many people stop here and think that this gives them all the information they need to understand what it means to be a woman.

Yet there is more to the story.

If we keep reading in Genesis 2, we see a more detailed account of the actual creation of man and woman. While

God made men and women equally human and in His image, He went about the process of creating them in entirely different ways. When we study this, we can't help but ask why.

The fact that God made Eve anatomically different from Adam does not explain why He made Adam first and later made Eve. After all, He could have created them both at the same moment and told them He had created their bodies differently so they could produce children. But He didn't.

He formed Adam out of the dust of the ground and placed him in the garden to work it (verses 7,15). Then, later, He made Eve from a rib He had taken out of Adam's side and brought her to him (verses 21-22). Yet, He made them both in His image and told both to rule over the earth. I believe that in verse 18, God answers the question as to why He created man and woman in different ways. After making the man and placing him in the garden, God said, "It is not good for the man to be alone," and then He said, "I will make a helper suitable for him."

I don't believe that Eve was an afterthought. We know

God knows all things. He knows the end from the beginning (Isaiah 46:10). He knew about the coming of Christ before He created the world (1 Peter 1:20). God knew He was going to make woman, but I believe He allowed Adam to be alone so that he could discover his desire for someone like himself—someone with whom he could share intelligent conversation and life and work; someone with whom he could be intimate and share his heart; someone who could respond to him and admire him and take joy in his accomplishments.

So God brought all the animals and birds He had created to Adam for him to name, but Adam did not find a suitable helper among them. So God put him into a deep sleep, took a rib from his side, and formed Eve from it. He then presented to Adam this beautifully formed woman who was taken from his side (Genesis 2:20-22). She was just like Adam in that she was also human and had been made in God's image and yet she had been made from him and for him (1 Corinthians 11:8-9). I believe God made woman second and different from man in order to give us a picture, an insight that would help *us* understand

God's desire for a people similar to Himself whom He could love and who would love and respond to Him.

I began to understand the importance of our masculinity and femininity when I studied 1 Corinthians 11:7-9, which says, "He [man] is the image and glory of God; but the woman is the glory of man. For man did not come from woman, but woman from man; neither was man created for woman, but woman for man." When I first studied this scripture, I was surprised. My immediate reaction was, "Wait a minute, I love God. Aren't I His glory too?"

The answer to this question is yes. Everyone in the body of Christ reflects the Lord's glory (2 Corinthians 3:18). Men and women alike participate in bringing Him glory and in being a glory to Him on the earth. But, in my opinion, the Bible is communicating something specific here about how we wives should relate to our husbands. God has created us feminine so that we can be a glory to our husbands in the same way He wants His bride, the church, to be a glory to Him. To glory *in* someone means to be proud of and rejoice in that person. To give glory *to* someone means to bring honor and adoration. The word *glory* means "highest pleasure, satisfaction, and pride." So when we are a glory to our husbands, we bring them honor and adoration, highest pleasure, satisfaction, and pride. We also give the world a picture of what God desires His church to do for Him. Ephesians 5 explains what this should look like in marriage. In this passage husbands represent Christ and wives represent the church. A husband is to love his wife "just as Christ loved the church and gave himself up for her to make her holy, cleansing her by the washing with water through the word, and to present her to himself as a radiant church, without stain or wrinkle or any other blemish, but holy and blameless" (verses 25-27). He is told to love his wife as his own body. Who of us, as wives, wouldn't want this kind of attention and tender care? I know how much I appreciate it when Ted takes the time and effort to really listen to me, comfort me, and encourage me. It renews and refreshes me, like being washed or cleansed.

The passage goes on to tell us to respect our husbands and submit to them, just as the church is to submit to Christ. This is not a demeaning role; it is a purposeful role.

We are representing how God wants the church to respond to Him. *In other words, we are a glory to our husbands in the same way the church is a glory to Christ. This is the purpose for our femininity.* I think it helps us understand our romantic hearts—our longing to adore and be attached to someone we respect and admire.

A woman's femininity complements and corresponds to a man's masculinity. Masculinity is attracted to femininity and finds it very beautiful. Femininity is attracted to masculinity and is stirred with respect and admiration. I love it when my husband is manly and strong and decisive in the way he cares for our family and the church. It makes me feel valued and safe. And I think he likes it when I respond with admiration and support and a willingness to help him, regardless of difficulties. This shows him that I will stand with him.

Single women experience the fullness of their feminine attributes in the way they relate to the Lord. First Corinthians 7:34 explains this when it says, "An unmarried woman or virgin is concerned about the Lord's affairs: Her aim is to be devoted to the Lord in both body and spirit. But a married woman is concerned about the affairs of this world—how she can please her husband." For the single woman, God Himself is the masculinity her femininity corresponds to and complements. When we understand that everything we do and the attitudes we hold are meant to portray the church's right response to God, it changes the way we view submission and the other scriptures in the New Testament directed specifically to women.

It explains why wives are told to submit to their husbands as unto God. I know submission is difficult for many women. Many avoid the subject altogether, which is often due to past abuses or wrong teaching they or their husbands have received. Still, the Scriptures tell us to submit to our husbands, so we must learn how to do it. It helps when we understand what submission is and know its purpose.

Very simply, submission is a gift from one person to another. It can never be demanded. Servitude can be demanded or forced, but that is something altogether different, and it has a negative bearing on a relationship between two people. Submission, on the other hand, is a heart attitude. It means choosing to rein yourself in for the purpose of helping and encouraging someone else in his or her leadership. It requires tremendous self-control at times and demonstrates strength rather than weakness. When we submit ourselves to our husbands, we are willingly choosing to yield to their authority. We do this out of obedience to God. He is the One who tells us to submit to our husbands (see Ephesians 5:22, Colossians 3:18, and 1 Peter 3:1). As we do so, we are ultimately submitting ourselves to God.

Of course, we must not throw wisdom out the window. We can maintain a kind and submitted heart attitude, yet not follow our husbands into sinful actions. If your husband is trying to get you to do something you know is sinful, ask the Holy Spirit how you can wisely redirect the situation and respectfully decline. Remember, you are to first submit to God, then to your husband. Also remember that God is tender toward those with submitted hearts, especially women. First Peter 3:7 says, "Husbands, in the same way [with a submitted heart to God] be considerate as you live with your wives, and treat them with respect as the weaker partner and as heirs with you of the gracious gift of life, so that nothing will hinder your prayers."

It pleases God when we submit ourselves to our husbands and follow Sarah's example. When God called Abraham and told him to leave his country, his people, and his father's household and go to a distant land, Sarah went with him. Many years ago I was in a similar situation. At that time Ted and I were working with the youth at a church in Baton Rouge, Louisiana, that we loved. Everything was going well. It was our first experience working for a church, so we were laying our foundation in marriage and ministry together there. After we had been at the church six years, Ted and I took a trip to Colorado where he spent some time praying and fasting in a tent on the backside of Pikes Peak while I visited my parents. After we returned to Louisiana, Ted asked me to go for a walk one evening. While we were walking, he told me that the Lord had spoken to him while he was praying and fasting in Colorado. He said he felt God was calling him to Colorado Springs to plant a church.

When he told me this, I stopped in my tracks and

stared at him. I knew I was with him in whatever the Lord called him to do. I had committed myself to help him. Yet I was shocked. My first thoughts were, *We have big dreams here; we love working for this church; we've always thought if we ever left, it would be to go to someplace like Calcutta or Mexico City, but Colorado Springs! How can we tell our friends?*

Nonetheless, Ted was confident. He felt God had given him a vision for the city. I was not trying to resist him on this, but I was having to work hard to catch up to him in my mind and heart. I went to the Lord and asked Him to please speak to me about all He was showing Ted, but the heavens were silent. I kept asking day after day, "Lord please speak to me. I just want to hear something from You that I can hold on to, so I know we are doing the right thing. I need to know what to tell our friends." But God didn't speak to me. So based on the fact that I knew He wanted me to help Ted, and since He had called my husband to Colorado Springs, I chose to support his decision, let go of the relationships and dreams I had that were connected with Baton Rouge, and say, "I'm going with you. I am with you on this. I believe God has spoken to you. He has not spoken to me, but that doesn't matter. I am with you."

Then, with the blessing of our senior pastor and his wife and our friends, we drove off the church campus with our two young children and a U-Haul truck and headed to Colorado. From the moment we pulled away, I have never looked back. Now, twenty years after planting New Life Church in Colorado Springs, I could not be happier. I love what God has done here and how He has blessed our family. Certainly it has not all been easy, but the challenges have been minor compared to the greater joy of being where God wants us and doing what He wants us to do.

Since I've been here, God has spoken to me many times and has given me a vision for the well-being of our family and the women of our church. But when I prayed to Him years ago in Louisiana, He was silent. Yet because I knew from Scripture that I am added to Ted to help him, I submitted myself to my husband and followed him. All I did was say, "Okay, Ted. I am added to you; I am your helper. I am going with you." And the Lord blessed that decision.

I've heard it said that men bond with those who help them in fulfilling their dreams. I want to hold that treasured position in my husband's life, to be his helper and companion. My femininity was created for this. As I have purposefully added myself to Ted and his calling, dreaming with him, working with him, and sometimes sacrificing with him, I have reaped the rich reward of love and intimacy in my marriage. I have found this deeply satisfying as a woman.

As I have come to understand my value as a woman, I have gained the confidence to embrace who I am and to live my life with joy. All of the lessons I have shared with you have set my heart at peace as they have brought me to a place of fulfillment in God. Now my needs are met in Him, and I am free to look outward and to love others more—particularly my husband.

It is not good for the man to be alone.
I will make a helper suitable for him.

—Genesis 2:18

He [man] is the image and glory of God;
but the woman is the glory of man.

—1 Corinthians 11:7

5

Seeing Your Husband

How do you see your husband? Do your eyes light up when he walks into the room, because just looking at him delights your heart? Or do your shoulders shrug with the thought, *Oh no, here he is again,* as you deal with feelings of regret or shame or embarrassment?

Every wife is given the challenge of learning how to love her husband. When we first marry, we think this will be easy. After all, we are usually off to a good start with our hearts full of love and hope. Yet over the course of time, the pressures of life and unexpected difficulties sometimes work against us and wear away at our love. Even so, God tells us to love and respect this one man, our husband (Titus 2:4-5 and Ephesians 5:33), and it is up to us to learn how to do it. Sometimes it takes an act of our will to choose to love our husbands, and while we are doing so, we should choose to go the distance and learn to love them well. I don't know about you, but I want to do the best job I can at loving my husband, and I don't want anyone to love him more than I do (except God, of course!). But how we see our husbands affects how well we are able to love them.

I have never forgotten the day I learned a valuable lesson about how I am to see Ted. One Sunday, when he was a young associate pastor, he preached a sermon in which he described angels in a way that was contrary to what I had been taught. I immediately started feeling anxious and embarrassed over this. Even though this was a relatively insignificant point in his sermon, I was sure other people were judging him and thinking he was ignorant about angels.

After the service was over, while we were talking to the senior pastor and some of the other associates, I sought to cover Ted's mistake, but instead, I just drew attention to it. I blurted out nervously, in what I intended to be a teasing and humorous way, that "of course we all know angels don't travel about by flapping their wings." My comments were met with silent stares as everyone in the group studied me to determine my point. I suddenly realized that nobody else cared about Ted's insignificant comment. I was the only one. They had been talking with him about the more important content of his message and how they appreciated it. What I said was not only irrelevant, it was totally out of place. Those pastors taught me to ease up on my husband and to get my focus off the minute and onto the big picture.

Since that time I've sat with other women who were feeling some degree of anxiety while their husbands preached. I have sensed them wondering if their husbands were going to make a mistake or whether others were going to like them. When the sermon is over, I will usually tell them how well their husbands did and point out meaningful parts of their messages. These wives almost always ask, "Are you sure he did all right? Didn't you hear when he said that part wrong—or gave the wrong Scripture reference or made some other mistake?" I always assure them that no one cares about that stuff. We are all adults, and most of us have learned to overlook other people's mistakes in the hope that they will overlook ours. What is important is our husbands' sincere desire to teach the Word and help people. That alone is honorable. We can admire that about our husbands and enjoy them as they do it.

If your husband makes a mistake or preaches poorly, he doesn't need you to tell him so. He usually knows it. What he wants from you is sincere encouragement. He needs to be able to trust that you see his desire to serve God and that you respect and support him. None of us should want to emulate Michal, the daughter Saul gave to David to be his wife.

King David knew what it was like to be appreciated and seen with respectful, admiring eyes. He also knew what it was like to be scorned by a wife who saw him in a less honorable light. In 2 Samuel 6 we have the account of David bringing the ark of God into the City of David. It was a time of great rejoicing. "David, wearing a linen ephod, danced before the LORD with all his might, while he and the entire house of Israel brought up the ark of the LORD with shouts and the sound of trumpets" (verses 14-15). Michal was watching from a window as the ark entered the city. "And when she saw King David leaping and dancing before the LORD, she despised him in her heart" (verse 16).

David, who was full of joy, continued to worship God

and sacrifice burnt offerings and fellowship offerings to Him. Afterward, David was so happy that he generously blessed the people and gave a loaf of bread, a cake of dates, and a cake of raisins to each person in the crowd (verses 17-19). Everyone went home happy, including David.

But when he arrived home to bless his household, he was met by an unhappy Michal, who scoffed at him, "How the king of Israel has distinguished himself today, disrobing in the sight of the slave girls of his servants as any vulgar fellow would!" (verse 20). David responded with indignation, "It was before the LORD, who chose me rather than your father or anyone from his house when he appointed me ruler over the LORD's people Israel—I will celebrate before the LORD. I will become even more undignified than this, and I will be humiliated in my own eyes. But by these slave girls you spoke of, I will be held in honor" (verses 21-22). Later we read that Michal had no children to the day of her death (verse 23), and that God established David's house forever (2 Samuel 7:16).

How could things have turned out differently for Michal? For one thing, she could have been worshiping and rejoicing with David and everyone else. The entire house of Israel was present with David (6:15), so why wasn't she? Why wasn't she a part of something that was so important to her husband? Even if for some reason she had not been able to participate, she could have wisely and respectfully tried to see her husband's heart and chosen to share in his joy when he came home.

Instead, she missed the bigger picture. David was sincerely worshiping God with all of his heart, and this pleased God, but Michal was embarrassed over the way he was dressed and the way he was dancing uninhibitedly before the Lord. She wondered what people would think of his lack of dignity and probably worried about how that would reflect on her. But the people recognized David was a great and righteous king. They knew he had God's favor and that God had chosen and anointed him king. They appreciated that David was showing enthusiasm for God in the way he was worshiping Him and rejoicing over the ark coming to his city. They did not think he was undignified. They understood that his heart was full of joy, and they rejoiced with him. But Michal couldn't see past her own feelings to see her husband's heart. She couldn't see that everyone else was honoring him. She couldn't see that the things that mattered to her really didn't matter to anyone else, least of all David. His only desire was to please the Lord. Unlike his wife, David cared more about pleasing God than he cared about what other people thought. We need to do the same.

It is important for us, as pastors' wives, to see and know our husbands, and to find in them what we can love and respect. We must be careful not to despise them in their pursuit of serving God. Even if they make a horrible mistake or preach poorly, we can encourage them based on the loving and respectful way we see them. We can focus on the greater picture and join them there. That is what Abigail did.

Abigail was also David's wife, but unlike Michal, she admired him and saw his heart and knew how to wisely encourage the good that was there. That is actually how she got his attention and later became his wife. The story takes place during the time when Saul was pursuing and trying to kill David, who was hiding in the desert.

Scripture tells us that Abigail was an "intelligent and beautiful woman," but she was married to a foolish man named Nabal, who was "surly and mean in his dealings" (1 Samuel 25:3). While David was in the desert, he sent word to Nabal, asking for provisions for his men. David and his men had been protecting Nabal's shepherds while they were herding sheep out in the desert, so he thought Nabal would willingly repay him.

Nabal arrogantly responded, "Who is this David?... Many servants are breaking away from their masters these days. Why should I take my bread and water, and the meat I have slaughtered for my shearers, and give it to men coming from who knows where?" (verses 10-11).

When Nabal's response got back to David, he got angry. So he gathered about four hundred of his men to go and attack Nabal and his household (verse 13).

When one of the servants told Abigail what was happening, she lost no time gathering supplies and riding out to meet David. When she found him, she quickly got off her donkey and fell at his feet and said, "My lord, let the blame be on me alone. Please let your servant speak to you.... May my lord pay no attention to that wicked man Nabal. He is just like his name—his name is Fool, and folly goes with him" (verses 24-25). (This is not the part of the story you are supposed to identify with!) Abigail goes on to ask David to receive her gift of provisions for his men, and then she proceeds to really get his attention with her wise words.

She told him, "The LORD will certainly make a lasting dynasty for my master, because he fights the LORD's battles. Let no wrongdoing be found in you as long as you live.... When the LORD has done for my master every good thing he promised concerning him and has appointed him leader over Israel, my master will not have on his conscience the staggering burden of needless bloodshed or of having avenged himself" (verses 28,30-31).

Listen to how differently David responded to Abigail than he did to Michal. He was disheartened with Michal's ridicule, and he was indignant in his response to her. But because Abigail saw him and understood him, he spoke kindly and gratefully to her. He said, "Praise be to the LORD, the God of Israel, who has sent you today to meet me. May you be blessed for your good judgment and for keeping me from bloodshed this day and from avenging myself with my own hands" (verses 32-33). Abigail had wisely protected her household from bloodshed and David from an act that would have left a stain on his reputation and his conscience. He recognized the good she did for him and was grateful for her respect and kind wisdom. Shortly afterward, God struck Nabal and he died. When David heard this, he sent word to Abigail and asked her to become his wife (verses 38-39).

Notice that this is the same man, but each of these women saw him differently. One despised him and scoffed at him; the other saw his heart, recognized his calling from God, and honored him. Like Abigail, we need to be the ones who see the hearts of our pastor husbands; we need to be the ones who honor and protect them, and who bring them "good, not harm," all the days of our lives (Proverbs 31:12).

How you see your husband can have a powerful influence on how he sees himself. If you see him with eyes of love and respect and tell him what is honorable and wonderful about him, you will inspire him to rise up to be his very best. That's what Abigail did for David. But if you see your husband as a disappointment or even as a failure, you will discourage him so much that he may lose heart and fail. Sadly, I've seen this happen in many marriages—let's not let it happen in ours!

We choose how we see our husbands. If for some reason it has become difficult for you to respect yours, look for even the smallest glimpses of attributes in him that you can respect or love and encourage him in these. Say, "Honey, I appreciate the way you close the garage door and lock up the house each night. It really makes me feel safe." Or, "I noticed how patient you were with Mrs. Brown when she shared with you her latest ailment. I loved watching you pray for her." Affirm the things you really do admire about him, and he will feel encouraged to do more. This also will help you start thinking along the right track, which will lead to your discovery of more admirable things about him. Think about those things rather than his weaknesses. Think about him the way you would want him to think about you.

I can't stop myself from admiring my husband. I still remember vividly the night I fell in love with him. We were at a college retreat, and Ted was preaching to a group of student chaplains. As I listened to him, I kept saying to myself, "I love what he is saying and how he is saying it. I love how he thinks! I love how much he loves God!" I felt as if I could see his heart, and I just kept admiring everything about him. From that time on, everything I learned about him reinforced that this was a man I could respect. So when he asked me out on a date a few months later, I was ready with my answer. Now in the more than twenty-five years since that first date, we have faced many challenges. As I have already mentioned, we have learned how to love each other on a much deeper level. And I am forever grateful for the counsel of the Holy Spirit who has guided us along the way.

Just last Sunday, as I sat listening to Ted preach, it occurred to me how much I still love what he says and how he says it. I still love how he thinks. I love how much he loves God. I love him. And I smiled.

A wife of noble character is her husband's crown,
but a disgraceful wife is like decay in his bones.

—Proverbs 12:4

The wise woman builds her house, but with her own
hands the foolish one tears hers down.

—Proverbs 14:1

6

Building a Great Marriage

When Ted and I were planning our wedding and honeymoon, he was also preparing for a mission trip to Ghana, West Africa, where he would be spending the summer up until the time of our wedding. In fact, he was scheduled to return home from Africa the week before, so this meant that I had to do most of the wedding planning. Just before he boarded the plane, he called me to say good-bye and that he was sending me a brochure about a "great" honeymoon idea. He wanted me to look over it, and if I liked the idea, to make the necessary arrangements.

When the brochure arrived, I was appalled. Ted's idea of a great honeymoon was a week-long group camping and backpacking trip. Sure, we would do fun things such as river rafting and hot-air ballooning, but all with our group, with whom we would also share tents at night.

Since Ted had left the decision up to me and told me to do as I liked, I quickly booked us at an old Victorian hotel in the mountains of Colorado. When he got home, he couldn't believe I preferred that over the group camping adventure. That was our first clue that maybe we weren't as much alike as we thought we were and that it was going to take some time for us to grow together. This is the beauty and challenge of all relationships. We have to figure them out.

Most of us want to have great marriages, and regardless of the state our marriages are in now, they can be great if we commit ourselves to making them the best they can be. Granted, this won't happen overnight, as everything about a marriage relationship is a process. Each marriage is as unique as the two people in it. Ultimately it falls to us to think and pray and learn. We will try and fail many times. As we seek to knock off our rough edges and learn to communicate and connect well, we may talk too much or too little or say the wrong things or do the wrong things, but we will also learn a lot about ourselves—where we are weak, where we are strong, where we are too strong. In time we *can* learn to flow smoothly in life and ministry with our husbands. This, along with growing spiritually and emotionally, will lead to greater joy and intimacy in our marriages.

I have already told you a little about what I learned that led toward deepening the intimacy in my own marriage. As you'll recall, there was a time when I thought Ted and I weren't going to have any romance in our marriage, at least not by *my* definition. Just think about it—a group camping trip for a honeymoon? Of course, Ted and I loved each other as much as we knew how, and we both valued our commitment to each other. But compared to where we are today and the mature love we share, the buds were just starting to appear and the love we now know was just emerging.

It was not until I had spent a few years in the school of the Spirit, though, that things slowly started to change. As I was growing in my spiritual relationship with God, experiencing a deep transformation that produced an increased measure of the fruit of the Spirit, I started to notice a little more attentiveness coming from Ted. It was not the degree of romantic fervor I was dreaming of, but it was the beginning of growth, and growth is good. What I was learning, though, was that I had to be intentional about cultivating this growth. As wives we must always be conscious of this, not in a pressured, insecure sort of way, but in a way that keeps our relationship growing so we don't take it or each other for granted.

When I talk with young women who are hoping to marry someday, I tell them that they need to keep developing themselves. Then, even if they don't marry, they will be striving to reach their best potential, which will benefit them in their lives and their service to God. All of us need to grow and mature spiritually, develop intellectually, and take care of ourselves physically. Self-development and personal growth don't stop after we marry. We should keep on learning and stretching ourselves so that we remain engaged in and excited about life. When we do this, we gain a deep sense of satisfaction because we are fulfilling our God-given potential. And, as I discovered, a side benefit is that we will also be more attractive to our husbands!

Please, don't go overboard with this. People who are too focused on themselves and who strive to be perfect in every way, particularly physically, tend to alienate other people rather than draw them close, and this sends the wrong message as to what our values are. Instead, we need to develop a comfortable beauty for ourselves, inside and out, physically, mentally, and spiritually. And we need to maintain this beauty with a reasonable amount of effort so we can turn our attention outward, which is where it needs to be if we really want to be beautiful. True beauty emanates from the heart, so let it shine through. *As we wisely learn to balance our lives so we can grow and improve, we will be able to make positive contributions in life and in our relationships.*

Even so, spiritual and personal development do not happen automatically. The second law of thermodynamics, which states that everything tends toward entropy (disorder and decay), can happen just as easily in our personal lives and relationships as it does in the rest of creation. So we must be intentional in pursuing life and growth in ourselves and in our marriages. We will know we are succeeding in this if our lives and marriages keep getting better over time. I've often thought there is no stage in my life that I would want to go back to, because none was better than the stage I am presently in. In spite of the challenges each stage has held, I can honestly say my life and relationships keep getting better. I hope I can still say that when I am ninety!

One of the ways we need to seek to grow and develop is in expressing our love for our husbands. We need to learn what means the most to them. To do this we need to pay attention to what pleases them. We can then do our best to see that they can enjoy those things.

Sometimes this may mean we have to make compromises and adjustments, but that makes our actions mean that much more, because our husbands will recognize our sacrifice of love. For example, Ted really *likes* people, lots of people. He would enjoy having our house full of people all the time if he could. In comparison, I tend to be more private, and I'm more comfortable being with a few people at a time.

Ted sometimes invites a crowd over at a moment's notice. This used to send me into a panic. I would think I needed to rush around cleaning the house and preparing food and would get upset at him in the process. Then everyone would come over, have a wonderful time, and be so grateful that we had opened our home. Ted would look like the selfless servant, and I would feel ashamed of my self-centeredness. Then I realized that having people over like this is one of the things that really makes my husband happy, so I decided I should stop resisting and jump in and help him when he spontaneously invites guests to come over.

Rather than avoid what Ted enjoys because it is uncomfortable to me, I've figured out how to adapt to it. In fact, I've adapted so well that now I *prefer* crowds and last-minute entertaining. People know I have had little time to prepare for them, so they don't expect the house to be perfect or for me to have food prepared. This helps me relax and enjoy our guests. This is so much easier than several days of anticipation and preparation!

Now, if we have a really big crowd, I sometimes find a task to do—like making several big cobblers in the kitchen. This enables me to focus on the few who join me while I cook. However, making cobbler usually draws a crowd, and one summer evening fifty college-age adults squeezed into my kitchen to enjoy the aroma of peach cobbler. Through the crowd I could see my husband enjoying me. Our eyes kept meeting, and he kept smiling at me. I could feel his pleasure. He appreciated that I was joining him—even helping him—in what he loves.

I found out that this kind of entertaining really isn't that hard after all, and the rewards of my husband's admiration and attention are a delightful surprise. Not only has this "sacrifice" earned his admiration, it has also made him want to be with me, which is what leads to intimacy.

For many women, learning how to express love to their husbands in a way that is meaningful to them will include learning to enjoy their sexual relationship. This is because for many men romance equals sex. In their minds the physical connection is the sincerest expression of love and the best way to be romantic. For most women, however, romance equals intimacy and a heart connection that is different from a physical connection—though it might include the physical. Both perspectives are valuable to the marriage relationship, and they go hand in hand with creating the *oneness* that scriptures such as Genesis 2:24 and

Ephesians 5:31 talk about. As Matthew 19:5-6 says, "For this reason a man will leave his father and mother and be united to his wife, and the two will become one flesh. So they are no longer two, but one. Therefore what God has joined together, let man not separate."

This *oneness* is intended to be far more than a legal description of how we can now function in society. It has real meaning for our hearts and souls and physical bodies. God created us for relationship. He wants us to figure out how to make our unique relationships rich and deeply satisfying. Remember, in our marriages we are picturing the kind of relationship God desires to have with us—not a legally binding union, but a life of shared love, communication, and intimacy.

When it comes to the sexual relationship, husbands usually show the greater enthusiasm. Men typically have the stronger physiological drive, and putting it off or out of their minds is not as easy for them as it sometimes is for us. When I asked my friend, author and speaker Lorraine Pintus, what she would say to pastors' wives, she put it this way, "Your husband needs sex. AND he needs romance. He needs you to admire him as a man, to adore him, and to affirm his prowess as a lover. He needs you to meet his physical needs. You are the only one who can minister to him in this way!" As wise women, women who are trying to build great marriages, we need to understand this and seek to express our love for our husbands through sexual love.

This includes recognizing that the sexual relationship in marriage is not just about our duty as a wife. I was stunned the first time I heard a young woman, whom I was counseling prior to her marriage, refer to sex as her "wifely duty." She told me her mother had taught her that sex was a miserable experience she would just have to endure. I had no idea mothers were still teaching their daughters such things! We need to teach women in our churches that sex in marriage is meant to be a mutually satisfying act of love.

In their excellent book *Intimate Issues,* Linda Dillow and Lorraine Pintus list six biblical reasons God gave the gift of sex to married couples:

- the creation of life
- intimate oneness

- knowing one another
- pleasure
- a defense against temptation
- comfort.*

I encourage you to read their book for a thorough explanation of the reasons God gave us sex. Each is mentioned in Scripture, and interestingly, sex for pleasure is mentioned most frequently. But all of these reasons provide wonderful benefits to the marriage union.

So we are wrong if we treat the sexual aspect of our marriages as insignificant. It is critical when it comes to marital happiness, and it brings its own reward. Most important, God designed sex as a means of unifying a husband and wife. It is a physical picture of intimacy, of becoming one. Thus, it is in our best interest—not to mention the best interest of our husbands—to figure out how to have and enjoy great sex.

Unfortunately, a lack of intimate affection is a common problem for many couples in ministry. Linda Dillow and

---

* Linda Dillow and Lorraine Pintus, *Intimate Issues* (Colorado Springs: WaterBrook, 1999), 6-10.

Lorraine Pintus have shared with me that as they travel around the country speaking about *Intimate Issues,* many pastors' wives say that their sexual relationship with their husband is nearly nonexistent. Lorraine met with one wife who admitted that she and her husband had not had sex in seven years. The wife told her, "Every Sunday Jeff gets up to preach. Every Sunday I sing on the worship team. We look like the perfect couple following God. But what happens when we leave the church and go home? Nothing. We sing and preach of love, but our marriage is a sham."

Before going any further, I must say that I understand this can be a painful subject for many women. Premarital or extramarital sexual activity, spousal involvement in pornography, betrayal, sexual dysfunction, wrong teaching or no teaching, and the many forms of abuse are just some of the reasons why the sexual relationship is so difficult for many women. Even so, the Word does offer us hope for our rescue and healing. With God's help we can overcome these difficulties and go on to have a great marriage, which includes a healthy and satisfying sexual relationship.

We must determine in our hearts that we are not going

to let our past define our future. We must believe that God not only forgives us, but He also cleanses and heals us. He alone is able to separate our sins from us and heal us of those sins and the subsequent wounds inflicted on us. If your past haunts your present, meditate on Psalm 51 until it becomes a part of who you are.

We must do everything we can to make our marriages great. It is necessary for the well-being of our families, and it is also the greatest gift we can give our congregations. We must guard our marriages and make them strong. Doing so will add to the health and stability of our churches and will serve as a model of a strong, intimate marriage relationship for others to follow.

If you long for more intimacy in your marriage, don't give up. Even if you have been waiting a long time, continue to ask God for His help, and remember that He will satisfy you with His intimacy in the meantime. God wants us to have a great and happy marriage, so don't settle for anything else. Determine to press in and take hold of His healing for you. Seek Him for His help and follow His counsel. It will be well worth the effort.

Just knowing that we must go through a process to grow and become mature can help us hang on during difficult times—like when there is miscommunication, lack of money, sexual problems, or sin that must be dealt with. People who give up too soon never learn that greater intimacy and fulfillment in marriage are usually just on the other side of that mountain they are facing. They just need to stay in the process until they get to the other side. When we recognize the Holy Spirit as our Guide, and go to Him and His Word for counsel, we will find that He will help us and give us the ideas we need.

So, is there hope for greater intimacy and romance in your marriage? Yes. Your marriage can be as intimate and romantic as you and your husband make it. You just need to take the time and go through the process of growing together. When you commit yourself to this journey and allow the Holy Spirit to be your Guide, you will receive the reward of rich fulfillment, satisfied hearts, and a great marriage.

*For this reason a man will leave his father
and mother and be united to his wife,
and the two will become one flesh.*

—Ephesians 5:31

7

Being a Devoted Mom

When our disabled son, Jonathan, was about thirteen years old, he was growing increasingly difficult to handle, and I thought I was reaching the end of my ability to care for him. He has always struggled with speaking clearly, yet he wants to talk like everyone else and to be understood. Nothing frustrates him more than when we can't understand him. As he was getting older, he acted out his frustrations by breaking things and striking out at his brothers. We could hardly get through a meal without Jonathan jumping up from the table, screaming, and throwing things, either because he couldn't participate in the conversation or because something else frustrated him that he couldn't communicate to us. It saddened Ted and me that in the midst of our vibrant, talkative family, we had a son who suffered so much. Yet in his suffering, he struck out at everyone else.

This had been going on for quite some time when I decided we all needed a break—a few quiet evenings, a little peace with our other children who had been patient and compassionate with their brother. What I felt we needed was not a permanent break, just a few nights a week. I thought perhaps there might be a school Jonathan could attend where he would stay through the week and then come home on weekends.

Understand, this was a major shift in my thinking. I never thought I would get to the place where I would be willing for Jonathan to spend time away from home. But I had become desperate for a little relief, and I was concerned for our other children.

So Ted and I made an appointment at Children's Hospital in Denver to discuss Jonathan's situation with a psychologist there. When we arrived, we sat down in her office, and Jonathan sat in my lap, curled up with his face hidden in my shoulder. After going over a brief description of what we were going through at home with our son, I finally got up the courage to tell her why we were there. This was extremely difficult as I sat there holding Jonathan, feeling ashamed and sad that I didn't think I could manage him anymore. I told her about his violent outbursts, his frustrations, the effect all this was having on our family, and that we needed a break. I asked if she knew of any residential schools in the state where Jonathan could stay and just come home on weekends. All the time I was speaking and crying, Jonathan stayed curled up on my lap with his face buried in my shoulder. I wished I didn't have to say these things in front of him, but he clung to me and wouldn't leave me. My heart was torn and broken.

The doctor studied me as I spoke, and when I finished she looked me squarely in the eye and said, "No one is going to love him like you do."

Those words slowly sunk into me.

When she said, "No one is going to love him like you do," it was as if God was speaking through her to me. In that moment I felt a renewed strength to love Jonathan. Suddenly I knew I could stretch a little more. I looked her back in the eye and said, "You're right," and we took him home.

After that it seemed Jonathan got easier to handle. Of course, he had been listening to that whole conversation, and it probably shook him up a bit. But in reality, I think I changed. I felt God had stretched my heart to love Jonathan more. Even though he still had incidents of frustration followed by outbursts of anger, we all seemed better able to manage them.

A few years later Jonathan communicated to me that he wanted to go to a different school than our neighborhood public high school. This surprised me because he has always loved school. I remembered that years earlier I had jotted down information about a special residential school that was in a different state. I had placed it in a drawer and had forgotten about it until Jonathan started saying he wanted a change. Suddenly I remembered it, and once we found the information, I called the school to find out more about it. Everything I was told sounded perfect for Jonathan.

So Ted and I took him to visit the school. At that time Jonathan was "into" fire hydrants, and he had been longing all summer to open one. He kept asking us whether the school would have them. Once we arrived, the first thing we noticed as we drove onto the school grounds was several big green fire hydrants. When we got out of the car, Jonathan started running around and jumping up and down in his excitement over them. When we met with the school director, Jonathan grabbed her hand and pulled her over to a fire hydrant. She smiled and asked, "Jonathan, do you like fire hydrants?" He squealed, "Yes!" Then she said, "Well, we use our fire hydrants to water our lawns, and we are in need of a man to open them for us."

Jonathan exploded with excitement—and I cried. He was so happy. God had answered his prayers. We knew he was in the right place.

He's been at that school two years now. We visit him often, and he comes home for holidays and summer vacations. He loves it. He feels grown up and more independent now that he is away at school. And he feels twice blessed that he has two homes.

I hope my journey with Jonathan is more extreme than anything you have faced or will ever face, although I know many of you are in similar circumstances. Even so, in hindsight I wouldn't trade the experiences I've shared with my son for anything. I love him deeply, and the process of growing in my love for him has made me a better, more compassionate person.

Nonetheless, I know that in some way, your children will give you opportunity to grow. Nothing in life stretches us more than being a mother. Motherhood causes us to face our weaknesses and can motivate us to try to overcome them. Most of all, it gives us the opportunity to learn how to love deeply and sacrificially—and learning to love this way is a sure path to personal maturity, and it provides ample opportunities for spiritual growth along the way.

Each of my children has contributed far more to my life than I ever dreamed when I became a mother. It really has not been all about what I have given to them. Motherhood for me has been filled with rewards. It has given me faith, wisdom, and encouragement to pass along to others. I don't want any of us to miss the valuable experience of motherhood with our children, both for their sakes and ours.

So it is important that you, as a pastor's wife, give yourself permission to place your responsibilities as a mother over and above any responsibilities you have at your church. Being a great mom is a more important contribution to the body of Christ than anything else you do—other than loving your husband. It not only sets an example for others to follow but also helps build a healthy family, which is a foundation of strength from which you and your husband can minister.

Just as we have to work out our relationships with our husbands, so we have to work out our relationships with our children. While there are many helpful books on parenting, each child is unique, so it is up to us to seek God through the study of His Word and prayer to know how to raise each of our children. When we depend on Him for wisdom about how to parent each of our kids, He will not disappoint us. Let me explain what I mean.

When our daughter, Christy, was in high school, she was facing some difficulties. I felt my role as her mother was to help her be strong and work through them, so I kept pushing her to do what I thought was right. Then one morning as I awoke, I felt the Holy Spirit telling me to listen to Christy. So later that day, I asked her to come into my room. When she did, we sat down together and I said, "Talk to me."

She told me what she had been going through, and I started to see that rather than force her to go through the situation, I needed to do what she was asking and remove her from it. When I told her this, she started to cry and hugged me. She said, "I've been praying that God would tell you to listen to me."

From all appearances, I was doing the right thing by pushing my daughter to face her difficulties and press through them. But the Holy Spirit counseled me to do otherwise. He knew what my daughter needed better than I did, and I needed His counsel to do the right thing. My listening to her that day opened the door for her to participate in a series of life-changing mission experiences overseas, all of which required more strength than the small mountain I was trying to force her to overcome at home. It also opened a new door of trust between us, which has continued to stay open these many years since.

Our oldest son, Marcus, loves learning and has already surpassed me in many areas of study. Throughout his years of growing up, he has had numerous questions about spiritual matters that haven't always been satisfied by my simple answers. Even so, I've always encouraged him to pursue God for the answers. I've even told him that God is big enough to handle his doubts and that if he would respectfully present them before Him, God would lead him to the answers. At times I've felt the Holy Spirit check me and tell me not to answer Marcus with the answers that satisfy me but to let him search them out for himself. I have been able to watch with amazement as the Lord has drawn Marcus to Himself, and today Marcus, a mathematical economics major at Colorado College, is preparing for pastoral ministry.

Marcus also loves life and nature. Outdoor sports are his passion. He especially likes mountain climbing, and because we live in Colorado, the mountains are close at hand. There have been many nights when I have had to release my worries to God and trust His care when I've known our son was out on a mountainside sleeping in a small tent, buried in snow, or possibly hanging from a rock somewhere. Even though I know what these experiences mean to my son, I don't think I would have allowed him to be so adventurous had I not learned to trust that my children's lives belong to God.

Our son Alex, who is quiet and thoughtful, is younger than Jonathan and has probably been impacted the most by having been raised with a special-needs brother. When we felt God leading us to allow Jonathan to go to school away from home, we were thinking of it as being for Jonathan's benefit. It never occurred to us that it might also be for Alex's. Soon after Jonathan was settled in his school, we started to see new sides to Alex's personality. We discovered he had this wonderful sense of humor and such insightful things to say. We also began to see and appreciate the quiet strength Alex brought to all the members of our family. I felt the Holy Spirit show me that not only had His attention been on Jonathan, it had also been on Alex. He knew Alex needed this. Even so, Alex is the one of my children who keeps a picture of his brother Jonathan up in his room and has written to him the most.

Elliott, on the other hand, is his own whirlwind of life and personality. He loves and fights with equal gusto. If it wasn't for the Holy Spirit's counsel, I would sometimes forget how very tender his heart is and how much he needs respectful, thoughtful, and kind counsel and attention. Sometimes I practically have to hold him still to give it to him, but the Holy Spirit assures me from time to time he needs it.

These are just small glimpses of the different kinds of counsel the Holy Spirit has given me in dealing uniquely with each of my children. As pastors' wives, hearing God's voice concerning our children, whether through the Word or during prayer, may be the key that enables us to raise healthy children who love God.

Being a good mom not only means depending on God for guidance in raising our children, it also means protecting them from unrealistic expectations that others may have of them. As parents, it's our job to create safe havens for our children so they can enjoy being kids and pass through the natural stages of development—physically, mentally, and spiritually.

We must protect our children from those who expect them to behave perfectly as though they were small adults.

We can do this, in part, by teaching our congregations how to rightly view the raising of children, ours included. We can let them in on the fact that children are going to make mistakes; it is inherent in the growth process. Sometimes they will even make bad choices. One of the roles of parenting is coaching our children through their mistakes and bad choices to help them learn wisdom. We need to encourage the parents in our churches to enjoy their children, which from time to time involves coaching and discipline but also includes patience and lots of love and laughter. Our goal as good parents should be to keep connected enough with our children so they will receive our coaching and not resist it.

Also, because we are in Christian leadership, some people may expect our children to have a spiritual maturity that is superior to that of other children their age. Many look to the pastor's kids to set an example for the other kids in the church. Once again, we must protect them from this type of thinking. Let me explain what I mean.

A couple of our kids did not like participating in the children's church program at our church. Even though it was a great program, they preferred staying with me throughout the service. After numerous disastrous and embarrassing attempts at forcing them to go to their respective classes, I decided it was not important to me that they set an example for other children in the church. That can be a heavy burden to place on the small shoulders of our kids. Instead, I was more concerned about my children loving church. For these two it took sitting with me for them to be happy in church. Eventually, their friends had a greater draw on them, and they looked forward to joining up with them and going to youth meetings. But I still relish the times when all my kids want to sit with me during the church services.

Another opportunity I had was to protect our son Elliott from undue pressures that had to do with expectations some of his teachers had for him to learn memory verses. This used to be one of Elliott's least favorite things to do. When he had a verse to memorize, he would avoid learning it at all costs and then struggle and fret over it the night before his test and totally forget it the next morning. His teachers would hint to me that surely a pastor's son should do a better job of learning his memory verses. But I was more concerned that he would begin to associate his dislike of memorizing verses with the Bible itself. Our ultimate goal was to teach him to love the Scriptures, so my husband and I began to just encourage him in the joy of reading his Bible and tried to take the stress out of it.

Since that time, Elliott has developed a relationship with a wise teacher who has created a very appealing reward system for learning Bible verses. Elliott is now in second place in the class for having learned the most verses, and he is striving to be first.

From the time our children were young, Ted and I have been praying that God would draw each of them individually and uniquely to Himself. More than anything, we want each one to genuinely know and love God. We want their experiences in God to be real to them and to have personal, life-transforming meaning. So we have not forced them down a precharted course for their spiritual growth. Rather, we have watched for opportunities to encourage them spiritually when they ask questions or show interest.

The best way we can encourage our children to have a relationship with God, however, is to set a good example for them. This is the best form of teaching. Let your children see you sincerely loving God and loving the church, His body. Let them see you attempt to live your life in a way that pleases the Lord. If you fail, let them see you make it right. Let them know you love God's Word, that it is light and life to you, and that prayer is valuable to you.

One morning when our daughter was home from college, she got up early and came into the living room where I was reading my Bible and praying. She said, "Mom, this will always be one of my fondest memories of you, seeing you sitting in this chair, in this room, reading your Bible and praying." What Christian parent wouldn't be thrilled to hear this from their child?

Our children bless us in many ways: They stretch us and help us mature and grow wiser, they bring us joy as we delight in their individual personalities, and they can bring strength to our lives and ministries as they mature in the Lord.

If you are struggling with a difficult or wayward child,

don't lose heart. Never stop loving and praying for your child. Keep seeking God for His counsel in how to deal with that child. He loves your child even more than you do and will be faithful to guide you. He also loves you and will give you peace and reward your heart in unimaginable ways as you continue to trust Him and seek His guidance.

Not long ago I flew back with Jonathan to get him settled at his school after he had been home for the holidays. We had a quiet and pleasant plane trip, playing games and writing little notes to each other. Once I got him settled, I asked him if he wanted to spend the last night with me in the hotel before I returned home. He did. After getting ready for bed, we decided to watch a humorous children's movie. We were each sitting up against stacked pillows on our beds as the movie started. But then Jonathan got out of his bed and crawled into mine. As he sat next to me, he put his arm around me and leaned his head over on my shoulder and stayed that way throughout the movie. We laughed a lot during the movie and just enjoyed those peaceful, happy moments together.

As the movie played, I reflected on all we have been

through in our relationship—all the struggles and hidden blessings. He's grown up a lot and so have I. What a gift God has given me in Jonathan. He knew I needed him— as I have needed all my children.

Parents are the pride of their children.

—Proverbs 17:6

Her children arise and call her blessed.

—Proverbs 31:28

8

Enjoying Friends

I used to think having friends was a nice but not necessary addition to a full and meaningful life in ministry. Being a somewhat private person, I was content, not to mention busy, just devoting myself to the relationships in my family. I believed, and still do, that my husband is my best friend, and beyond that my relational energy needed to be spent on my children. The rest of my relationships were friendly and cordial, but not as close as they could be. I thought life, as I knew it, was a pretty full cup.

What I didn't realize was that I was slowly becoming a dry well. I was unaware that I was missing the whole river of women's relationships that God had intended to fill me up. Certainly, God was my deep inner source of fulfillment, and He kept me satisfied during my times with Him in prayer. Yet I was missing out on another channel He wanted to use to strengthen my life: other women in the body of Christ. It wasn't until God spoke to me about leading our women's ministry and I started spending time with the women in the church that I discovered how very valuable these relationships could be.

Women can understand and affirm each other on a feminine level, which can strengthen and encourage us. Think of the strength Jesus's mother, Mary, and her cousin, Elizabeth, brought to each other during their pregnancies and the births of Jesus and John the Baptist. God gave each of them a task that neither of them could fully comprehend. He gave them wonderful, supportive husbands, but He also gave them each other. They must have giggled with delight behind closed doors as they shared each other's joy and marveled over God choosing them to take part in the most wonderful miracle of all time. They must have also encouraged each other's faith. Just knowing they were both going through similar circumstances had to strengthen them as their pregnancies progressed.

That's what we women do for each other, and that is why we need each other. We help each other become better, happier, more godly women. Even we pastors' wives need friends who will help us to do this.

In chapter 1, I described one of my favorite paintings of a group of women joyously bringing in the harvest together. For me this picture depicts the joy of serving God with others. It's true that each of us stands alone before God in our individual relationships with Him and in our obedience to Him. But our work in serving Him is best done through our connections with others. This is why Romans 12:4-8 calls us a body made up of many members with each one doing his or her part. It is also why Jesus commands us to love one another and why the world is to identify us by this love we have for each other (John 13:34-35).

Jesus does not give us this command to create a burden for us. We are not supposed to spend our lives struggling to love other members in the body of Christ. Rather, He wants us to experience the strength and joy of relationships. He knows that when we learn to love each other and work together, we will experience greater joy as we bring in the harvest (see Luke 10:2).

Shared work and shared joy creates friendships. True friends strengthen our lives. Proverbs 18:24 says, "There is a friend who sticks closer than a brother." This type of friend is joined to you not by flesh and blood but through shared life and purpose. This is why we will find our greatest friendships among those with whom we share life; most often these people are within our own churches.

Sadly, many seem to hold the view that those in pastoral leadership should not form friendships with those in our own congregations. They believe we should look outside of our churches, particularly to others also in pastoral leadership, to find our friends. I disagree. I believe it is a misconception that pastors and pastors' wives cannot have friends within our own congregations. That is where we need them most!

Certainly, after more than twenty-five years in ministry, I have many good friends who are pastors' wives or who serve in other forms of ministry all over the globe, but my closest friends are the ones I do life with. They are in our church; they are our community. Most of them are either married to men on our staff or have joined me in other forms of ministry in the church. God has put us together in a body of believers made up of many members so we will connect and draw strength and joy from each other as we serve Him. In each of our congregations are women who love God and want to mature in their relationship with Him. These women can be our friends. It is a rich part of life to develop friendships among those we do life with. Our church should be our community of friends.

Of course, we must be wise in choosing our friends, especially our closest friends and confidantes. Everyone should. It takes time to build intimate relationships—to get to know someone, to discover if they have true faith, if they are walking with the Lord, and whether they share a common purpose with us. Over time we discover those among us who are trustworthy, who earn our respect, who we naturally connect with, and who bring us strength and joy.

I feel surrounded by a great company of friends in our church who offer me kind support and encouragement. Many of them are women I know I could be closer to if only we had the time and the energy. Even so, a few have emerged whom I am especially close to and with whom I am more comfortable sharing my life and my dreams on a more intimate level. These women share a common purpose with me: They love the church and help me in women's ministry. We've been friends for many years now, and I know they are godly women, trustworthy women, faithful women. They are women I respect and admire, love and trust, and who love and trust me.

Three of them came alongside me as I wrote this book. They spent time every week praying for me throughout the process and met with me weekly to encourage me and add joy to my life and labor. Just thinking about them makes me smile. They also strengthen me. They think more highly of me than I do of myself, and they encourage me to do my best. I can't imagine my life without friends such as these with whom I can do life and ministry.

It's also a good idea to share in friendships as a couple. Together Ted and I find our closest friends are those within our church who help us in ministry. Many of them are on our staff, but there are others who have just come alongside to help and to share life and ministry with us. Since Ted and I have given our lives to serving God, we don't have much time or energy to focus on close relationships outside of the context of our purpose. What we have found is that relationships that share a common purpose happen naturally and are the easiest to maintain—and they make ministry more fun.

When people share life and ministry together, they become friends. We see this with Jesus and His disciples. He surrounded Himself with a group of men and did life with them. They lived together and ministered together. They bonded through their common experiences and purposes and became friends. Jesus led from within, in the midst of His friends. He led those He had relationships with. He lived with them, and in doing so, He encouraged leadership abilities in them. We can follow His example by developing relationships with the women in our churches and rallying them around us like a team. They will be much more interested in following us if we value them and see ourselves as one of them. It is a "we" mentality rather than an "I" and "you" mentality.

I think some pastors and their wives are afraid that if they become friends with those on their staffs and in their churches, people will become too familiar with them and no longer respect their leadership. Jesus, however, didn't seem to hold this perspective. He lived with those He most wanted to influence. You don't have to worry about whether others will respect your leadership as long as you are confident in your leadership and lead wisely. If you are living your life in a manner worthy of respect and are following God's counsel in your leadership, others will respect your position. But they will also love and support you more if you value and respect them. This is the basis for friendship.

We also needn't worry about what other people will think if we draw closer to a few friends. This will happen naturally. Jesus did this with Peter, James, and John. Rather, we should use the opportunity to set an example of friendship for others. Let people see you enjoying your friendships. It can encourage them in their friendships. Just keep your relationships godly and inclusive rather than exclusive. In other words, be friendly to everyone, regardless of the level of your relationship with that person.

Also, allow for an ebb and flow of close friendships

and be open to relationships changing with seasons. Some women will be our close friends for life, and others will be close for certain seasons. Always welcome a broad range of friends and let the women of your church know you see them as friends. Just be wise in selecting your closest friends and confidantes. Trust God's leadership in this. I always watch for those God is adding to me rather than looking for close friends myself. The friends God brings into my life are usually the people who come alongside me, and who I can see, over time, share a common purpose and calling with me. We just end up doing life together, and our relationships grow naturally.

While there are risks inherent in all relationships, the value of having relationships should outweigh the fear of losing them or being wounded by them. Many pastors' wives fear that they will form a close friendship and then that person or family will leave the church. The saying "It is better to have loved and lost than never to have loved at all" holds true here. Loving others makes us better people. And remember, it is Jesus's job to build the church. Trust Him to place people where they need to be. It makes it easier to let them go. Also, don't close the door too tightly when they leave. They may very well be back, or you may discover the relationship continues on a different level, but you will have learned something about them in the process that will help you gauge what the level of your relationship should be.

Remember, you should view your husband as your very best friend. Never put another person above him in your heart. He is the one God has added you to, the person with whom you are one and who God tells you to respect and love. He is the one with whom you most share life and purpose. Never allow anyone to come between you and your husband, and never confide in anyone about your husband unless you are seeking help for your marriage from an older, godly woman.

But also enjoy women friends. They can increase your joy in life and add strength to all you do. Soon I will be meeting with a group of my friends to plan a tea that we want to do for the women of our church. Preparing for it with friends will be as much fun as the event itself. I'll probably meet some new friends in the process. I'm sure I will learn some new stories about women's lives, and we will have plenty of opportunities to pray for and encourage each other. I am looking forward to it. Thinking about it makes me smile.

A friend loves at all times.

—Proverbs 17:17

9

Being a Gracious Leader

S everal years ago I was embarking on my first attempt at coordinating the National Day of Prayer event for our city. I believed this day was important and felt God had laid it on my heart to facilitate a significant observance of it in our city.

I drove to a meeting to give a presentation to the leading pastors of our city, with the hope of enlisting their support. Knowing that my husband would be present made me all the more determined to do a good job so as not to embarrass either of us. I prayed all the way there that God would help me speak graciously and intelligently.

When I arrived, I was ushered into the room. All eyes were on me as I was given the floor. Everyone knew I was Ted's wife, so I am sure they were curious to hear what I was going to say and how I was going to say it. I wanted to be a glory to my husband that day and obey what I felt God had given me to do. So as graciously as I could, I explained to them that I wanted to serve them and our city by preparing a place for Christians to gather to pray for our nation. I appealed to them as the city's spiritual leaders to lead the event, and I told them that I would take care of all the preparations.

When I finished I felt their approval. I had won their favor, and they were willing to help make the event a success. Even more valuable to me, though, was the look on my husband's face. I could see and feel his pleasure with me. He was proud of me. I had been his glory.

No doubt, I was leading that day, but my leadership was not expressed through commanding authority. Instead, I used the position I held beside my husband to graciously influence others.

As a pastor's wife, you share in your husband's leadership because you are one with him, called alongside to help him, and because people are naturally going to be watching you. But your leadership is different than your husband's. After all, he is the pastor and carries the weight and authority of that position, but as the pastor's wife, you wield a lot of influence, even if you are at home rearing your children or prefer to stay out of the spotlight. How you use your influence can positively or negatively impact your husband's ministry and the church. As women, our leadership will be received if we are gracious and kind and seek to use our influence for the good of others. Let me explain what I mean.

As a young college student, I observed how this worked between our college president and his wife. I attended Oral Roberts University, a Christian university, and the founder, Oral Roberts, was still the president and the visible spiritual leader on campus while I was there. President Roberts was well loved and respected by our student body. His wife, Evelyn, was always close by his side and was also loved by the students.

I vividly remember one chapel service when President Roberts was fielding questions from the audience and a student questioned the need for a dress code. He received such a fiery retort from President Roberts that the whole student body was shaken. We all left chapel that day with mixed emotions. The talk multiplied in the dorms. Some were angry, while others defended President Roberts.

During the next chapel service, Evelyn stood before the student body and calmly explained what had seemed to us an extreme reaction by our president. She explained that he had fought hard to establish the university according to what he felt God had shown him. He was very protective of every detail in how the school was run. To him, this was a matter of obedience to God, and his fear of the Lord was the reason for his unmovable position in many of these matters. That is why he had rebuked this student so sternly when he questioned the dress code. It was an important matter to President Roberts because it questioned his obedience to God. He knew this, but we didn't.

As Evelyn spoke, we began to understand President Roberts more and why he did things the way he did. When she finished speaking, we all applauded her. We felt her respect and love, and through her wisdom, she made us feel safe. We also loved her. She had single-handedly rekindled our affection for President Roberts, and in the end, she had increased our respect for him.

Evelyn Roberts understood that because she was married to a leader, she, too, was a leader. She realized she could use her influence to strengthen and support her husband's ministry, and that's exactly what she did. She also knew how to do it. She was kind and gracious, which reached us on a heart level and enabled us to receive her leadership. She led us that day, not by usurping her husband's role, but through her influence as his wife. She wisely helped him and us. She was strong but revealed this strength through her gracious heart. It was easy to receive from her as a wise and nurturing mother.

We saw this type of womanly leadership again in Laura Bush, wife of President George W. Bush, after the September 11 attack on the United States. President Bush had declared war on terrorism, and tensions were increasing between the United States and Afghanistan.

During that tense time Laura Bush did something no one expected of her and what no other First Lady had done before her. On November 17, 2001, she addressed the nation using the entirety of the president's weekly radio broadcast time. During the program she revealed the plight of the women and the children in Afghanistan and appealed to our hearts to have compassion for them. She explained that our war on terror was against the type of regime that would deny women basic human rights and treat them so abusively.

Most of us are aware that in 2001 Afghanistan was

ruled by the Taliban, which had strong links to al Qaeda, the terrorist group that had attacked the United States. Afghan women were forced to cover themselves from head to foot in burkas and were not allowed to leave their houses unescorted. They were not allowed to receive an education, and those who had been highly educated prior to the Taliban takeover were denied the opportunity to use their skills. In fact, educating women or girls was punishable by death. Women who committed lesser offenses, such as wearing makeup or fingernail polish or showing their feet, could be punished by imprisonment or by having their fingernails pulled out.

In her radio address, Laura Bush led by teaching us to love those we could have considered our enemies. She wisely explained that the war on terrorism was not against the Afghan people but against those who would deny these people, particularly the Afgan women, their freedoms. She appealed to our hearts to see this war as a compassionate effort.

Our unsettled nation felt safe with Laura Bush that day. We sensed her strength and wisdom and were inspired by the kindhearted way she expressed it.

Both Evelyn Roberts and Laura Bush used their influence wisely. They stood with their husbands and helped them by their graciousness and kindness. This endeared these women to those under their influence and inspired many to respect their husband's leadership.

In contrast, I have seen wives of ministry leaders in churches or parachurch ministries who were disliked and even despised by those they influenced. In one such situation I overheard the wife of a parachurch ministry leader being referred to as the "Dragon Lady." Those who worked in this ministry dreaded her presence. She barked out orders and treated people harshly and with little respect. Even though these workers respected the leader, they wanted nothing to do with his wife. Many left that ministry because they grew weary of dealing with this woman. Even though her intent was to help her husband, she lacked the wisdom to know that her help would have been better received had she been kind and gracious.

We must never underestimate the power of a kindhearted woman. Proverbs 11:16 tells us, "A kindhearted woman gains respect." People appreciate and can receive from a woman who is kind. Kindness is not a weak character trait. Having it doesn't mean you try to please everyone or are sappy with mercy. Sometimes it takes tremendous strength and wisdom to be kind, and it can be a powerful tool for influencing our families and others for good. Kindness complements graciousness; it trains the tongue to speak graciously and creates gracious actions. It is respectful of others and seeks the best for them. As we saw with Evelyn Roberts and Laura Bush, it opens the door so wisdom can be imparted.

Queen Esther, whose story is told in the Old Testament book of Esther, offers us another excellent example of kind graciousness. When King Xerxes was searching for a new queen, Esther was brought to the harem along with all the other beautiful, young virgins from the king's realm. Esther stood out among all the young virgins. She was lovely in form and features. She pleased Hegai, the eunuch who was in charge of the king's harem, and he gave her special treatments. When the time came for her to go in to the king, she followed Hegai's guidance. The king was attracted to her more than any of the other virgins, and she won his favor and approval more than any of the others.

So he chose her to be queen. The fact that she won the favor of everyone who saw her or spent time with her tells us she was not only beautiful but must have been kind-hearted rather than tough, hardened, and harsh in her dealings with others. Also, the way she submitted herself to her cousin and guardian, Mordecai, as well as to Hegai and, ultimately, to King Xerxes himself reveals a gentle, submitted, and kind heart.

But Esther was not just a pretty ornament for the king. Her husband not only loved her, he also respected her. When she sought his audience, he responded to her. He even offered her up to half of his kingdom. She did not take advantage of this, but graciously appealed to him on behalf of her people. She knew she was placed in her position for a purpose, and she used her womanly strengths to wisely petition her husband and, ultimately, rescue her people from genocide. Because she was gracious, respectful, and wise, the king trusted her. She was able to influence him for good.

As pastors' wives we can do what Laura Bush, Evelyn Roberts, and Esther did. We can seek to develop kindness in our hearts, which will not only endear us to our husbands but will also enable us to use our influence in a way that strengthens and complements our husbands' effectiveness. Gracious women earn an open door to influence others through their kind consideration and respect. As pastors' wives we can have a positive impact on our churches and even on our world if we are wise to this truth.

A kindhearted woman gains respect.

—Proverbs 11:16

10

Smiling at the Future

We recently had a leadership conference at our church with attendees from all over the world, and I spoke to the wives of the ministry leaders. Our hearts connected as I told my stories, and I could see hope in their eyes. Even though we discussed some of the struggles we commonly face, I could see that these women were not willing to be classified among the poor, pitied, burned-out brand of pastors' wives who dread the very role to which they have been called. Instead, they were full of hope for their future. They understood the value of our calling.

I am glad to be among them.

As I walk down the halls of our church on a Sunday morning, I don't feel animosity or fear or that I have to fit a certain persona. People greet me and seem happy to see me, and I am happy to see them. I know they love me and pray for me and my family. I love them and pray for them as well. We belong to each other. We are a family.

I believe that all pastors' wives can enjoy this kind of relationship with the people in their churches. Scripture asks the same of us that it asks of all Christians: that we live our lives sincerely before God. This is the kind of life that is worthy of respect, and when we earn the respect of others, we will often also earn their love. This deepens our relationships and enhances the joy of ministry.

Our congregations are looking to see how we live out our faith, so we must be sincere in the process. If a pastor's wife feels as if she has to maintain a facade, then she can't help others understand what it means to take their concerns and difficulties to the Holy Spirit for counsel. They won't ever observe how God can enable us to transcend difficult circumstances and experience joy and freedom in Him. This is real life in God.

As we mature in God, we gain wisdom that can keep us from becoming burdened and trapped by the expectations others may have of us. For instance, Scripture never tells us that we must attend every church service, wedding, funeral, wedding shower, and baby shower. Nor does it tell us that we must dress impeccably and sit on the front row, play the piano or sing in the choir, lead the women's Bible study, listen to everyone's complaints, treat everyone equally and impartially—which may mean not having close friends because that would be showing partiality—or cheerfully receive less-than-urgent phone calls at our homes, day or night, and not mind that everyone has equal access to our husbands' time and attention. Most of these expectations have become part of our church cultures, yet they have no biblical basis and place unnecessary burdens on us and on our husbands. If we seek to meet unbiblical expectations such as these, we'll do our churches a disservice by allowing our congregations to remain immature and dependent on us.

We'll also wear ourselves out.

When we try to meet the demands God never intended us to meet, we'll become overwhelmed and eventually burn out. These burdens rob us of the joy of ministry, which is all about leading people to Jesus, teaching them the Scriptures, and helping them mature in their relationships with God, their families, and the body of Christ. But if we hold our ground with graciousness and strength of heart and do only the things we know God has given us to do, then we will grow stronger in the eyes of others and be better able to lead them by our example. We will be an encouragement to all who are watching us to see how to live a godly life.

I walk down the halls of our church happy, not because this is how I am supposed to act, but because I have learned to walk in freedom. You can, too, if you will seek to do the following:

- Build an intimate relationship with the Holy Spirit and go to Him for counsel.
- Understand that God sees you, and your life counts to Him.
- Value your femininity and the uniqueness of your role in marriage and in the body of Christ.
- Love your husband well.
- Take delight in your children.
- Enjoy godly friendships.
- Develop kindness so you can be a gracious leader.

I hope that after reading this book you will understand

that we can't do all of this overnight. Growth is a process and a journey. But if you will join me in embracing this journey, you will find joy, wisdom, and freedom—and you will smile at the future.

*Strength and dignity are her clothing
and she smiles at the future.*

—Proverbs 31:25, NASB